YOUR ONE WILD AND PRECIOUS LIFE

The Audacity to Curate a Life You Love

MIA ROSE DUNLAP

MYND MATTERS

Mynd Matters Publishing
2690 Cobb Parkway SE
Ste A5-375
Smyrna, GA 30080
www.myndmatterspublishing.com

978-1-963874-14-3 (pbk)
978-1-963874-15-0 (hdcv)

FIRST EDITION

To your
inner life:

When we are quiet enough to listen, it is guiding us. Witnessing us. Hugging us with its words. Preparing and warning us.

What's Inside

Introduction

This book is for 3 categories of people:
1. People who are starting their journey of reflection and healing.

2. People who are in transition—career, family, living, etc.

3. People who are committed to their healing work and want to deepen it.

Over the past four years, social media has been the platform where thousands of followers engaged with questions that ranged from the last time they were held to when they first fell in love with their favorite ice cream flavor. The questions are used to both be a platform for folks to pause and reflect and to remind folks that we are not alone.

This journal takes users on an exploration—a voyage, if you will, to examine our lives to examine our habits and opens a door to an opportunity to know and to see what is happening already such that it's possible to keep doing it with intentionality or to change it, if you want.

You will be in the company of hundreds of thousands of people who have invited self-care into their lives. In some ways, *The Audacity to Curate a Life You Love* is about self-care—but it does not give answers. It is not a self-help book that gives you tips or tells you what to do. Instead, it takes you back to your center, your inner guru, your own light and instincts.

Sometimes we go looking for answers when really, our life is calling us to stop and LISTEN to the truth that's screaming within.

Who were you before your trauma? How did you get here? What did your inner voice say to you? How do you hush your inner critic? What is the inner critic saying anyway? What does it want?

I imagine that while going through the questions within this book, many emotions will arise. Without being prescriptive, I invite you to pause...and listen to them. Your feelings may be communicating some important information that you need to know about yourself, about the question, or something else. Be open to listen.

In Rumi's poem, "Guest House," he says, "a joy, a depression, a meanness, some momentary awareness comes as an unexpected visitor // welcome and entertain them all // be grateful for whoever comes, because each has been sent as a guide."

I am journeying alongside you. At the start of each chapter, I give you a peek into my world and share my personal response to the first prompt. My hope is that this journal will support you in pausing to listen to what comes up for you as you read and respond.

There is no one way to do life and there is no one way to take the journey through these pages. You may pick a question a day, you may respond to a section a week, you may do this alongside someone or in a small group, you may not have a specific rhythm or beat to which you take this journey—however you decide to journey—trust that you are choosing from the best place within you.

Curating Your Relationship with

Yourself

No one is you, that is your power.

– Odessy

Finish this sentence: I wish I would have had ____ in childhood.

I need to define childhood as 0-22 (lol). I wish I'd joined a sorority in college and studied abroad and joined a pageant. Those all still hold weight for me. I was overwhelmed and felt like I was breaking barrier after barrier and being the first in my family to do X, Y, and Z, but I was tired. My sophomore year of college, I wanted to go back home to Chicago because I felt like I was betraying my two younger siblings by leaving them to fend for themselves without me...in abject poverty with parents who struggled with illness.

Ugh, I'm getting choked up writing this.

I know so many people could say that's not my responsibility or I was helping by being an example and blah blah blah. But I am PAINED still that I couldn't be who they needed then. I'd call home, "Hey, how y'all doing? I am going to send you some underwear and shirts for school, ok?" I chose to focus on making it to the other side of poverty and achieving and it worked.

It worked until I realized I had blind spots around maintaining vulnerable and soul deep relationships. Sure, I can rationalize the reason I chose to go headfirst into achievement because of poverty and not wanting to repeat the cycle. But, my goodness, do I wish I'd learned how to love deeply and how to be loved well...sooner.

Finish this sentence: I wish I would have had ___ in childhood.

....

....

....

....

....

What are important parts of caring for yourself that you want to focus on?

....

....

....

....

....

What is your journey with mental and emotional health?

....

....

....

....

....

What are examples of being in love with yourself?

....

....

....

....

....

How has your relationship with yourself changed over time?

....

....

....

....

....

What's your personal superpower?

....

....

....

....

....

What is your love language? How do you speak it to yourself?

....

....

....

....

....

What is your ideal relationship with yourself? How does it look? Feel? Sound?

....

....

....

....

....

What questions do you have for yourself right now?

....

....

....

....

What do you want to keep in mind from this chapter?

....

....

....

....

....

Curating Your
Life
Team

If you want to go fast, go alone.
If you want to go far, go together.

– African Proverb

What's been the most significant relationship in my life?

Hmmm...a lot of thoughts came up for me. First, I thought, it would be powerful to say to myself, but for some reason that doesn't resonate right now.

Then I thought of saying my mom and all the ways I needed to be close to her but also feel resentment, so does that make it the most significant or the most complex?

Then I thought about my therapist and my aunt Barbara—they are my rocks. Or is it the woman I fell in love with although I am not gay? That relationship healed me in ways I didn't know existed.

It's hard to choose one but if I have to for the sake of this question, it would be the one with survival. The only way I knew to live was to survive. Learning survival methods from pretending the pay phone was broken to getting quarters from people walking by to storing my stolen clothes in my school locker so they wouldn't be stolen, worn, or sold at my house. I learned to eat syrup bread for breakfast and ketchup sandwiches when necessary—it was often necessary. Survival taught me to keep my head up and pretend (really well) that everything was ok because that's what survivors do.

When I began the journey to end my relationship with survival—I ached. For eighteen years, it was my lifeline and ten years to follow—I used everything it taught me. But I needed a new way to live. This is my most significant relationship.

Describe the most significant relationship in your life:

....

....

....

....

....

Who are the three closest people to you? Describe them in one word.

....

....

....

....

....

What role does each of those people play in your life? In which areas of your life do they have significant impact?

....

....

....

....

....

....

....

....

....

....

What values are most important when curating your team of people who are closest to you?

....

....

....

....

....

Describe how you show up in your most significant relationships.

....

....

....

....

Who else would you want in your inner circle / life team? Why?

....

....

....

....

....

What questions do you have for yourself right now?

....

....

....

....

....

What do you want to keep in mind from this chapter?

....

....

....

....

....

....

....

....

....

....

Curating Your Relationship with
Pleasure

Ask not what the world needs. Ask what makes you come alive and do that. The world needs more people who come alive.

– Howard Thurman

What are you naturally good at?

I think I am better at writing than I am speaking although I am really good at both. Speaking is easier and faster to do, so I prefer it.

When I write, I bleed. I let myself fall apart in my writing, trusting that afterwards I'll be able to put myself back together. Trusting that when the writing ends, I will be ok. I don't think I can do that if I speak and let the words ooze from the chaotic and unkept part within me. I'm not always sure I will be able to pull myself back together. Not always sure I will be able to stop the bleeding. What if I start hemorrhaging as I am speaking? Then it's public and shaming and bad and ugly and...NOPE. I won't do it. I will get close though. I can get close to my pain when I am speaking. That's what makes me as effective as I am. I just can't touch a wound, especially an open one.

What are you naturally good at? How often do you do it?

....

....

....

....

....

....

....

....

....

....

What brings you pleasure in your life?

....

....

....

....

....

How will you make time for pleasure this week? Month? Year?

....

....

....

....

....

In your ideal world, how would you describe recreation and fun in your life?

....

....

....

....

....

What questions do you have for yourself related to curating your relationship with pleasure?

....

....

....

....

....

What do you want to keep in mind from this chapter?

....

....

....

....

....

....

....

....

....

....

....

Curating Your Relationship with
LOVE

Love will make you crawl out of your hiding place.

What is your current relationship with love?

When I was a kid, I used to be the "good girl." I learned that "being good" got me so much love and positive attention. In school, at my Upward Bound and after school programs, at church—I was everyone's favorite. They'd say, "I would LOVE to have a daughter like you." They always said they saw something special in me. So, I fell in love with being seen and known and loved from the inside out.

My parents both struggled with addiction illness throughout my childhood—so that kind of love and adoration was not available at home. And by some miracle, I chose to see it in some of the best places ever—and I am all the better for it.

It was love that kept me alive all those years when I used to cry in my pillow, "God if you love me, you'd let me die tonight." But love woke me up, love made sure I made it to school and back safely. Love. So my current relationship with love is: it loves me back...it follows me everywhere I go...and I love it!

What is your *current* relationship with love?

....

....

....

....

....

....

....

....

....

....

What is one of your favorite love stories (that you've experienced)?

....

....

....

....

....

What are lessons you've learned about love?

....

....

....

....

....

What questions do you have for yourself about love?

....

....

....

....

....

What is your *ideal* relationship with love? How does it look, feel, and sound?

....

....

....

....

....

Curating Your Relationship with
Money

Money is only a tool. It will take you wherever you wish, but it will not replace you as the driver.

-Ayn Rand

What early lessons did you learn about money?

Usually when I hear the word lesson, I think about "positive learning experience," but *my* only honest answer to this question is that I learned all the hardest lessons about money.

Lesson 1: Money is tight

Lesson 2: Money is divisive—I've witnessed relationships end and people at their ugliest from having borrowed money, needed money, and had money.

Lesson 3: if I have too much, I'll be a pawn, an ATM, or a disgrace forever saying no. Conversely, if I have too little, I'm a liar and worthy of being searched in my sleep.

Lesson 4: It's a sin to love it except that every pastor and preacher I've known seeks it almost desperately.

Lesson 5: Money is the cause of the biggest heartbreak in my life—being homeless at fifteen. It was money that tore my life apart.

What early lessons did you learn about money?

....

....

....

....

....

Describe your current relationship with money.

....

....

....

....

....

How has your money story changed over the years?

....

....

....

....

....

What are your money habits—saving, spending, investing, *etc.?*

....

....

....

....

....

Who in your life has a healthy relationship with money? *Describe what this means to you.*

....

....

....

....

....

What would you change about the way you engage with money?

....

....

....

....

....

If you had the money you want right now, how much would it be? Why that number?

....

....

....

....

....

What questions do you have for yourself right now?

....

....

....

....

....

What is your ideal relationship with love? How does it look, feel, and sound?

....

....

....

....

....

....

....

....

....

....

Curating Your Relationship with
Fear &
Failure

Life is 10% what happens to you and 90% how you respond to it.

– Charles Swindoll

When was the last time you tried something and felt like you "failed" at it?

Three years ago, I offered a pre-order for a different version of this journal. Back then, I was self publishing. In doing so, I collected over $2,500. But I felt like an imposter. What if people didn't like it or it had errors in it or something else was wrong that I couldn't think of?

The questions—the fear—paralyzed me and I didn't finish what I started. I sent everyone their money back and didn't respond to any messages for days as I cried myself awake every morning.

When was the last time you tried something and felt as though you "failed" at it?

....

....

....

....

....

....

....

....

....

....

What lessons did you receive about fear and failure?

What's something you're proud of related to your relationship with failure?

....

....

....

....

....

What are some lessons failure and fear taught you?

....

....

....

....

....

What is something you're currently doing that's scary but you're doing it anyway?

....

....

....

....

....

Describe your ideal relationship with fear and failure.

....

....

....

....

....

What do you want to remember from this section?

....

....

....

....

....

What questions do you have for yourself?

....

....

....

....

....

Curating Your
Wellness
Journey

The best six doctors anywhere and no one can deny it are sunshine, water, rest, air, exercise, and diet.

– Wayne Fields

How do you feel about your body?

When I was ten or eleven, my butt protruded through my clothes and my shape was defined and curvy and appealing. In school I was constantly reminded that I was dark. Not "pretty to be dark skin," but that I was midnight, blue black, burnt, and even called ugly. The boys in school teased me and the men outside the school preyed on me.

Men felt like they knew what to do with a "body like mine"—or so they'd say. I was an oxymoron, a perplexing poem, a distant melodic sound.

I seemed irresistible to men twenty years my senior and shunned by boys my own age. My body didn't protect me. So, I covered it. In baggy pants and too long shirts.

I've since learned to take care of my body and see it as a friend that has its own voice and value. I learned to listen to it rather than what others say to and about it. I learned to live in my body.

How do you feel about your body?

....

....

....

....

....

What/Who has informed your reflection of yourself?

....

....

....

....

....

What are your current wellness habits and rituals?

....

....

....

....

....

**If you could tell your body anything loving,
what would you say?**

....

....

....

....

....

If your body could talk, what might it say back to you?

....

....

....

....

....

What do you want to do a better job at as it relates to wellness?

....

....

....

....

....

What secrets or resentments are you carrying in your body?

....

....

....

....

....

Whose wellness journey do you admire most? Why?

....

....

....

....

....

If you were to describe your ultimate experience with health and wellness, what would it be?

....

....

....

....

....

....

....

....

....

....

....

What do you want to remember from this section on wellness?

....

....

....

....

....

....

....

....

....

....

....

Curating Your Relationship with your Legacy

Legacy is not [always] leaving something for people, it's leaving something in people.

–Peter Strople

What is your reputation right now?

- Inspiring but inconsistent

- Hard to read

- Fierce—I take risks

- I ask questions that get at the heart of things

- I am healing and am vocal about the process

Describe your reputation:

....

....

....

....

....

....

....

....

....

....

....

Who has a legacy that you admire? What do you admire most about their legacy?

....

....

....

....

....

....

....

....

....

....

....

Who are the people who left something in you?

....

....

....

....

....

What are you most proud of in your life so far?

....

....

....

....

....

What do you regret or wish you'd done differently in your life?

....

....

....

....

....

In your ideal world, what would be true of your legacy?

....

....

....

....

What do you want to remember from this section on legacy?

....

....

....

....

....

....

....

....

....

....

Curating Your
Healing
Journey

You may not control all the events that happen to you, but you can decide not to be reduced by them.

– Maya Angelou

Who is guiding you? How do you know?

Wellll...that depends on the day. I would love to say the Divine is guiding me. And on most days, I think it is. I know because I see signs and feel Its presence closely and deeply. I know because I ask for Its guidance and see the manifestation of Its help...and I make spiritual meaning from what I experience, and I can't help but think it's the hand of the Divine. So, who—the Divine—most days.

Other days, it's my instincts, my trauma, my feelings, my rage. It's ME. I know because I ain't asking and I ain't listening for many answers from the Divine. I move. I choose. And sometimes it works and other times I feel like I've ended up in sinking sand.

Who is guiding you? How do you know?

What parts of you are hurting?

....

....

....

....

What makes you feel safe?

....

....

....

....

....

With whom do you feel safest?

....

....

....

....

....

What is confusing or even scary about your journey?

....

....

....

....

....

When was the last time you spoke to yourself lovingly?

....

....

....

....

....

What outstanding questions do you have for yourself?

....

....

....

....

....

What do you want right now from your life?

....

....

....

....

....

What are your next steps on your healing journey?

....

....

....

....

....

Describe your life when you have healed the aching part of you? How will you know it's healed?

....

....

....

....

....

....

....

....

....

....

....

Curating Your Relationship with
Time

The bad news is time flies. The good news is you're the pilot.

– Michael Altshuller

What are you pretending not to know about the way you spend time?

I am pretending not to know that my lack of discipline is in the way of my actual success. As I am not intentional with my time, I am not intentional with my life. It is all connected.

I am pretending that I don't know what is in my way. If I really got honest, besides the obvious answer of "me," I would say the thing that's in my way is fear of isolation. Missing out. Fear of loneliness. What if I work extremely hard and get really far, and no one is there with me? I am not even fully realized now, and the experience is already a lonely one. So why would I work harder to be successful?

Wait.

Am I not productive with my time because I fear success?

What are you pretending not to know about the way you spend time?

....

....

....

....

....

What takes up most of your time? Do you want to keep it that way?

....

....

....

....

....

What habits do you need to change to see a difference in your life?

....

....

....

....

....

What habits are working for you? How do you know?

....

....

....

....

....

What are your 3 biggest distractors?

What can you do to alleviate the distractions?

....

....

....

....

Who can you trust to hold you accountable to doing what you said you would do?

....

....

....

....

In your ideal world, how would you describe how you'll use time to support in your productivity (write in the present tense)?

....

....

....

....

....

....

....

....

....

....

What do you want to hold on to from this section on time?

....

....

....

....

....

....

....

....

....

....

Curating Your Relationship with
Home

You are home in you. You will live there for the rest of your life. Make it a beautiful place.

Home is the most tender and authentic part of me. It's the place where I can "be" without having to consider "what ifs" or "what was."

Home feels like a warm bath, a sweet embrace. I find it in me but I also find pieces of home in the people who love me...and love me well.

Home has not always been a safe place for me. I can remember the first time I ran away from home when I was 13. I ran and ran and ran...not sure what I was looking for, but I knew I couldn't stop running until I found it.

I spent years running until I gave myself permission to stop. I began to build a home that I loved returning to, both physically and emotionally. With support from my therapist, I continue to make my home my favorite place to be. And to be the reflection of the kind of home I always needed.

Who or what is an embodiment of home for you?

....

....

....

....

....

When was the last time you were "home"?

....

....

....

....

....

In what ways is your physical home a reflection of who you are?

....

....

....

....

....

What items in your life represent the feeling of home?

....

....

....

....

....

What does your ideal home look, feel, and sound like?

What do you want to hold on to from this chapter? What questions do you have about home?

....

....

....

....

....

....

....

....

....

....

About the Author

Despite enduring significant childhood trauma, **MIA ROSE DUNLAP** proudly graduated from Spelman College in Atlanta, GA making her a first-generation high school and college graduate. Mia Rose attributes her success to her village of angels on Earth that were safe havens (programs and people), therapy, and her own courage to color outside the lines.

During her journey at Spelman, she spent her ten-week summers doing internships across California, Washington DC, and Atlanta as a youth advocate for children who had suffered deep pain much like herself.

After earning her bachelor's degree from Spelman, Mia Rose moved to New York City where she earned her master's degree, became a teacher, principal, and later a director of culture for schools. She started a motivational speaking and life coaching company, AYA: Adversity Yields Audacity, with the vision to empower young adults to beat the odds and curate a life they love.

At age 28, she curated a solo "sabbatical" and backpacked three months through Europe and ended it with a seven-day silent retreat in Portugal. She speaks about the journey on "The Audacity Show," a talk show she created for people to share their journeys of overcoming adversity and shattering glass ceilings.

In Atlanta, Mia continues to work in education as a culture consultant, life coach, and hosts creative and soulful experiences. Her favorite quote is, "So tell me, what is it you plan to do with your one wild and precious life?" by Mary Oliver.

You can reach Mia Rose at www.miadunlap.com and Instagram @The_audacity_of_Mia_Rose.

Additional Thoughts

Additional Thoughts

Additional Thoughts

Additional Thoughts

Additional Thoughts

Additional Thoughts

....

....

....

....

....

....

....

....

....

....

Additional Thoughts

Additional Thoughts

Additional Thoughts

Additional Thoughts

www.ingramcontent.com/pod-product-compliance
Lightning Source LLC
Chambersburg PA
CBHW051546120626
46551CB00013B/1385